Make in a Day

CENTERPIECES

Amy Bell

Dover Publications, Inc.
Mineola, New York

Bibliographical Note

Make in a Day: Centerpieces is a new work,
first published by Dover Publications, Inc., in 2017.

Library of Congress Cataloging-in-Publication Data

Names: Bell, Amy, 1981– author.
Title: Make in a day : centerpieces / Amy Bell.
Description: Mineola, New York : Dover Publications, Inc., 2017.
Identifiers: LCCN 2017001914| ISBN 9780486813691 | ISBN 048681369X
Subjects: LCSH: Table setting and decoration. | Centerpieces.
Classification: LCC TX879 .B445 2017 | DDC 642/.6—dc23
LC record available at https://lccn.loc.gov/2017001914

Manufactured in the United States by LSC Communications
81369X01   2017
www.doverpublications.com

CONTENTS

As the daughter of a gifted seamstress and an accomplished oil painter, my home as a girl was always brimming with creativity. There is no doubt that the act of creating has helped shape my life, starting with those early days of watching my mother at her machine and my father at his easel.

All grown up now with four children of my own, I have never outgrown that creative gene. My life's passion is to teach others to harness their unique creative talent, because I genuinely believe everyone has the ability to create something to be proud of with their own two hands. My blog, Positively Splendid, was founded in 2010 out of that passion, and since then, I have been honored to reach millions of people with step-by-step, accessible craft tutorials that have empowered makers of all experience levels to pursue their own creative journey.

On the pages of this book, I have curated a selection of my very favorite centerpiece designs, all of which can be completed in just the span of an afternoon with supplies easily found at any craft store. With ideas suitable for lively occasions, from birthdays and baby showers to formal events like weddings and dinner parties, it is my hope that reading this book will inspire you to create a beautiful display for your next special gathering.

To all of you—regardless of whether you have been a maker all your life or if you are just embarking on your path of creativity—welcome! I am so excited to have the opportunity to make beautiful things together.

To creativity,
Amy

P.S. I would love to hear from you! I invite you to send photos of your projects that are inspired by this book to Amy@PositivelySplendid.com, and they might just make a cameo on PositivelySplendid.com!

Stacked Fishbowl Centerpiece

Our family's favorite vacation destination has always been the beach. We love to walk along the shore together picking up shells we find along the way. This stacked fishbowl centerpiece is a lovely way to showcase those special finds! This centerpiece would be perfect for a beach wedding, or for a casual summer dinner party with friends. I love that the shells and other elements can be swapped out as desired to give this display an entirely different look in just a matter of minutes.

To make this centerpiece, you will need:

* Large fishbowl for the base tier
* Small fishbowl for the top tier, the base of which fits snugly into the opening of the top bowl without falling through
* Multi-surface craft paint
* Adhesive craft stencils
* Foam pouncer
* Decorative sand in two colors
* Assorted seashells
* Decorative rocks, stones, or other items
* Pillar candle (optional)

1. Wipe the outside and inside of each of the fishbowls clean with a lint-free cloth. Apply the stencils to the outside of the bowls in the desired configuration, and then stencil the design using the craft paint and foam pouncer. Remove the stencil while the paint is still wet, and set the bowls aside to allow the paint to dry completely.

2. Fill the larger fishbowl with a 1" layer of the first sand color. Pour the second sand color over the first to create another 1" layer.

3 Arrange assorted shells and stones on top of the sand in the larger bowl until you achieve a look you like. You can also add other found elements such as beach glass or small driftwood pieces for a rustic look.

4 Carefully stack the two bowls together so the base of the smaller fits into the top opening of the larger. Fill the smaller bowl with sand as you did in Step 2.

5 Arrange shells, stones, rocks, and other elements in the top tier, working carefully so you don't displace the items in the bottom tier. If desired, add a pillar candle to the top tier to give the finished centerpiece a romantic glow.

Farmhouse Chic Centerpiece

This Farmhouse Chic Centerpiece exudes rustic charm, but it is anything but old-fashioned. Flea market finds that incorporate barn wood and other elements from days gone by are a great way to add character to today's decor projects, and the great news is that the items you need to get this vintage look are available at any craft store! This centerpiece is a perfect option for an outdoor wedding or any other casual, yet sophisticated, gathering. Filled with greenery and flowers of your choosing, it can be tailored to suit any color scheme or theme.

To make this centerpiece, you will need:

* Unfinished wood crate
* Acrylic craft paint in two colors
* Foam brush
* 220-grit sandpaper
* Lint-free cloth

* Stencils
* Stencil brush
* Floral foam
* Serrated knife
* Artificial flowers and greenery
* Iridescent cellophane

1 Use the foam brush to paint the entire surface of the crate, both inside and out. Apply as many coats as needed for even coverage, allowing paint to dry for 15–20 minutes between coats. Set the crate aside to dry completely.

2 Use the sandpaper to gently sand away some of the paint at the corners and other areas to give the crate an aged, antique look. Wipe the crate clean with the lint-free cloth.

3 Using the stencils, stencil brush, and the contrasting paint color, create a design on the front of the crate as desired.

4 Use the serrated knife to trim the floral foam so that it fits inside the bottom of the crate.

5 Arrange the artificial flowers and greenery as desired by tucking the ends of each piece down into the foam.

6 Tuck small pieces of the cellophane down into the crate around the floral foam so that the foam isn't visible from the outside of the finished centerpiece.

Decoupaged Can Centerpiece

Taking an item that otherwise would be discarded and turning it into something beautiful is one of my favorite things to do from a creative standpoint. In this shabby chic decoupaged can centerpiece, humble aluminum cans are transformed into stylish vases with the help of a bit of paint, some pretty paper, and decoupage medium. Filled with fresh-cut flowers and greenery, these can be displayed individually or in a grouping for an abundance of colorful impact. When crafted in different color schemes and with different fillers, this same project can be tailored to any event or season, making this one of my all-time favorite centerpiece ideas for everything from weddings and baby showers to holiday table settings and more!

To make this centerpiece, you will need:

* Empty aluminum can(s)
* Multi-surface craft paint
* Paintbrushes
* Decorative tissue paper
* Decorative-edge scissors
* Decoupage medium
* Floral foam
* Serrated knife
* Fresh or artificial flowers
* Decorative stones or rocks
* Small chalkboard sign
* Ruler (optional)

1. To begin, thoroughly wash and dry the empty can. Using the paintbrush, apply two or three thin coats of the craft paint to the outer surface of the can, allowing the paint to dry 30 minutes between coats. Set aside to dry completely, at least three hours.

2. Using the decorative-edge scissors, cut a strip of paper long enough so that the edges of the piece overlap by at least ½" when wrapped around the can. Cut a wider or narrower piece, depending upon how much of the painted portion you desire to be visible above and below the paper strip in the finished project. For added precision, measure with a ruler before you cut.

3 Apply a thin layer of the decoupage medium to the back side of the paper piece using a paintbrush, making sure the decoupage medium is applied all the way to each of the outer edges of the piece.

4 Use the paintbrush to apply a thin layer of the decoupage medium to the outside of the can, working quickly to ensure the medium on the back of the paper piece doesn't dry as you work.

5 Affix the paper piece to the outside of the can, positioning the piece so it is centered. Carefully smooth the paper into place to remove any bubbles under the surface of the paper. If needed, brush on a bit more decoupage medium at the point where the edges of the paper overlap to ensure the piece stays firmly in place.

6 Use the brush to apply two thin coats of decoupage medium over the entire surface of the can, allowing the project to dry for 30 minutes between coats. Pay special attention to the border around the paper piece to prevent the piece from pulling away from the can later on. Set project aside to dry completely.

7 Using the serrated knife, cut a piece of the floral foam to fit snugly inside the can. If using fresh flowers and greenery, moisten the foam thoroughly with water.

8 Insert the stems of the flowers and greenery down into the floral foam in the desired arrangement. Cover any exposed foam with the decorative stones or rocks, and finish by inserting a miniature chalkboard with your chosen sentiment into the center of the arrangement.

Stacked Succulent Centerpiece

There is something so naturally elegant about succulents, and they are a perfect way to bring a verdant pop of color into any space. Live succulents are absolutely lovely, but there is also a terrific assortment of faux succulents available in many craft stores that allow you to achieve the same look without the fuss of caring for living plants. This stacked succulent centerpiece showcases artificial succulents in a uniquely beautiful way by placing them in tiered terracotta pots to give the centerpiece plenty of eye-catching height and dimension. This centerpiece would be perfect displayed on a round table for a dinner party or other gathering, as it is equally beautiful on all sides!

To make this centerpiece, you will need:

* Three terracotta pots in ascending sizes: one small, one medium, and one large

* One terracotta saucer to fit the largest pot

* Painter's tape

* Scissors

* Bottle of liquid gilding

* Paintbrush

* Floral foam

* Serrated knife

* Rock salt

* Assorted artificial succulents

1. Cut pieces of the painter's tape in varying lengths, and affix them on the outside of each of the pots, overlapping them to form various geometric designs. The entire surface of the largest pot should contain a design, but it is only necessary to apply tape to the top half of the outside of the medium and small pots, since the lower portion won't be visible in the finished project.

2. Using the paintbrush, apply the liquid gilding to the surface of the pots in the negative portion of the taped-off design. On the small and medium pots, only apply gilding to the taped top halves of the pots, and not to the lower halves, since these portions will be hidden in the finished centerpiece.

3 Use the paintbrush to apply liquid gilding carefully around the entire perimeter of the outer rim of the saucer. Set aside all of the painted pieces, and allow them to dry for at least 30 minutes.

4 When the liquid gilding is completely dry, carefully pull away the tape from each of the pots and discard. Set the pots aside.

5 Using the serrated knife, cut two sections of the floral foam to fit snugly into the bottom of the medium and large pots. Fit the foam pieces into their corresponding pots so they hold firmly in place.

6 Place the largest pot on the work surface, and then nestle the medium pot inside the larger so that the bottom of the medium pot is elevated by the foam piece inside the large pot. If necessary, trim the foam piece in the large pot slightly so that it allows about half of the medium pot to be visible above the top rim of the large pot. Stack the small pot inside the medium pot in the same way.

7 Starting on the bottom tier and then working up, fill the openings in each of the pots with the rock salt, filling to about ½" from the top rim of each level.

8 Carefully insert the stem ends of the succulents down into the rock salt to anchor them into place, trimming away a portion of the stem with scissors, if necessary, so the entire stem can be submerged. Continue to arrange the succulents in this manner until all tiers of the centerpiece are filled.

Peppy Pinwheel Centerpiece

With four children in our family, there is never a shortage of celebrations around our house! As a mom, I love to make days like birthdays extra special with a handmade touch, but more often than not, I don't have an abundance of time to do so. The good news is, making decorations for kids' celebrations can be quick and simple, and especially so when you commission the assistance of little helpers. This peppy pinwheel centerpiece is bright, whimsical, and fun, and it is perfect for birthday parties, baby showers, and more. And because the pinwheel accents are so easy to create, this is a great centerpiece to make with kids so they can feel the satisfaction of helping with the party prep, too!

To make this centerpiece, you will need:

* Double-sided decorative paper
* Paper trimmer
* Scissors
* Pencil
* ⅜" glue dots
* 1" round paper punch
* 2" round paper punch

* Paper straws
* Hot glue gun and glue sticks
* Clear glass container
* Floral foam
* Serrated knife
* Jelly beans in assorted colors

1. Use the paper trimmer to cut a square from the decorative paper. (For the project seen here, two 5" x 5" squares and one 4" x 4" square were used.) Fold the paper in half widthwise and then lengthwise, so the larger square of paper is separated into four smaller squares. Mark the very center point where all of these squares meet with a pencil.

2. Use scissors to cut a diagonal from each of the four outer corners about halfway to the marked center point.

③ Place a glue dot directly over the marked center point. Working with one of the snipped sections, fold the section so the outer tip is aligned with the center dot. Press the tip firmly onto the glue dot to anchor it in place.

④ Continue to fold every alternating corner of the snipped sections up to the center point in a similar fashion. Press firmly into the glue dot to anchor the corners in place so that every other snipped section is anchored to the center point to form a pinwheel.

⑤ Use the 1" round paper punch to cut a circle from a contrasting piece of patterned paper. Apply a glue dot to the back of the circle piece, and press it down over the center point on the front of the pinwheel to conceal the place where the tips of each section meet.

6 Use hot glue to affix a paper straw to the back center of the pinwheel. Use the 2" round paper punch to cut a circle from a piece of paper that matches the back of the pinwheel. Use hot glue to affix the circle over the point where the paper straw is glued to the pinwheel to conceal the end. Repeat Steps 1–6 to create as many pinwheel accents as desired.

7 Use a serrated knife to cut a section of the floral foam to fit in the center of the glass container while leaving about ¾" open on all sides. Apply a small amount of hot glue to the bottom of the foam piece and affix it to the bottom center of the container. Insert the stick ends of the pinwheel accents into the foam, arranging them in the desired configuration.

8 Pour the jelly beans into the opening between the container and the foam piece to conceal the foam. To create an ombré effect, pour the jelly beans one color at a time to create striped layers of different colors.

Fringed Platform Centerpiece

There is something so festive about fringe, and it is a perfect way to add movement and texture to just about any project. In this fringed platform centerpiece, simple crepe paper streamers are transformed into fringed trim and then used to create a tiered centerpiece made from inverted hatboxes that can be used to display a word, message, or number. This centerpiece would be perfect created in a couple's wedding colors to display their new monogram, or it would be equally lovely at an anniversary celebration when used to display how many years the lucky couple has been married. Crafted in metallic colors such as gold and silver, it would be a fantastic accent at a New Year's Eve gathering as well. There are so many possibilities!

To make this centerpiece, you will need:

* Crepe paper streamers

* Scissors

* 3 papier-mâché hatboxes in ascending sizes; used here: 3", 4½", and 7½" in diameter

* Hot glue gun and glue sticks

* Decorative paper

* White glue

* Paper straws

* Twine or ribbon

* Wood word accent

1 Use scissors to cut a streamer piece that is approximately 24" long. Fold the piece in an accordion fashion.

2 With the section still folded, make snips from the bottom edge to about ½" from the top edge, spacing the snips about ¼" apart. Unfold the newly fringed piece and set it aside. Repeat Steps 1 and 2 to create three sections of fringe for the bottom tier, two sections for the middle tier, and one section for the top tier.

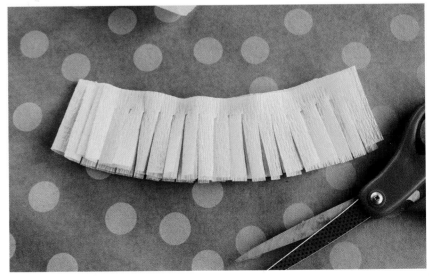

3 Working with one box at a time, use hot glue to affix the fringed strips in concentric circles around the box, working from the bottom of the inverted box (in this case, the open end of the box) to the top, placing the lowermost strip so that the fringe hangs over the bottom edge by about ½". Continue affixing the fringed strips, overlapping each one by about 1", until you reach the top edge.

4 At the top of the box, affix the final fringed strip so that it overlaps the top edge by at least ½", securing the fringe to the box with hot glue.

5 Trace the box lid onto a sheet of decorative paper, and cut out with scissors. Affix the piece to the top of the box with white glue to conceal the place where the top layer of fringe is attached to the top of the box. At this point, you can discard the lid, or set it aside for use in a later project.

6 Repeat Steps 3–5 to prepare the remaining two boxes. When each tier is complete, stack them in ascending order, with the largest box on the bottom and the smallest on the top, placing the tiers so each box is precisely centered on the one below. Secure the three tiers together with hot glue.

7 Use scissors to make a ¼" hole on either side of the lowermost tier, poking through the tier very gently so the box doesn't collapse or bend as you work. Insert a paper straw through each hole.

8 Secure the wood word piece in between the paper straws. To do so, cut two lengths of twine, and tie a piece onto each end of the wood word accent. Secure the other ends to the tops of the paper straws with a knot.

Wood Word Centerpiece

Sometimes an occasion is so special, you just want to shout it from the rooftops! This bold wood word centerpiece conveys just that level of excitement by showcasing a favorite word, monogram, or date in a bold, eye-catching way. I love that this centerpiece can be changed for any number of occasions easily and inexpensively by simply swapping out the letters in the display. This would be the perfect centerpiece for a graduation party when outfitted with the graduation year or a school's initials.

To make this centerpiece, you will need:

* Unfinished wood craft letters
* Acrylic craft paint
* Paintbrushes
* Jumbo craft sticks
* Decorative paper
* Pencil
* Scissors

* Hot glue gun and glue sticks
* Decoupage medium
* Craft foam
* Serrated knife
* Galvanized metal container
* Shredded paper filler
* Ribbon

1. Paint the entire front surface of each of the letters with two or three coats of the acrylic paint, allowing the paint to dry for 15 minutes between coats.

2. Paint the front and back surfaces of a craft stick in the corresponding color for each letter using two or three even coats, allowing the paint to dry for 15 minutes between coats. Set the letters and the sticks aside to dry completely, approximately one hour.

3 Position the letters onto the decorative paper (for letters that are not the same front and back, place the letter face down to trace in reverse), and trace around each one with a pencil. Carefully cut out each letter with scissors, trimming just inside the traced outline. Set trimmed letters aside.

4 Affix a craft stick to the back center of the letter in its corresponding color using hot glue, pressing firmly to secure. Repeat with the remaining craft sticks and letters.

5 Using a paintbrush, apply a thin layer of decoupage medium to the back of the trimmed letter paper piece. Apply an even layer of decoupage medium onto the back side of the wood letter piece, directly over the craft stick.

6 Place a paper piece onto its corresponding wood letter piece, carefully aligning all outer edges. Press to adhere, using your fingers to smooth out any wrinkles under the surface. Repeat with all of the remaining paper pieces and wood letters. Set the letters aside to dry for one hour.

7 Use the serrated knife to trim a piece of foam to fit snugly inside the galvanized container while leaving about 1" of space between the top of the foam and the rim of the container. Apply a small amount of hot glue to the bottom of the foam, and position it inside the container, pressing down to secure. Insert the stick end of each of the letters into the foam, in the desired order and position.

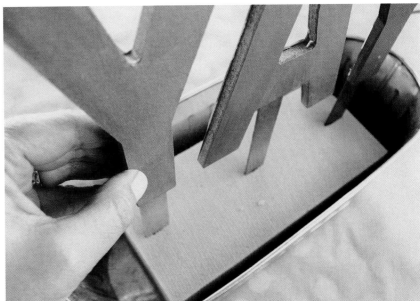

8 Fill the empty space above the foam piece with the shredded paper filler, concealing the bottoms of the craft sticks. Finish by tying a coordinating bow with the ribbon around the outside of the container.

Rustic Pedestal Centerpiece

Bringing a touch of nature indoors is such a great way to bring texture and warmth into a home. Natural elements like moss, stones, and wood are inexpensive and accessible; but when put together in this beautiful rustic pedestal centerpiece, the end result is homey, refined, and incredibly chic! This wood pedestal would also be lovely to display small mementos or photos, or even for creating a holiday display with evergreen cuttings and pretty vintage ornaments.

To make this centerpiece, you will need:

* 2 basswood circles of different sizes

* Felt

* Permanent marker

* Pinking shears

* Heavy-duty adhesive

* Wood candlestick

* Craft paint

* Paintbrush

* Moss

* Decorative stones

* Flameless pillar candles

1. Place the larger basswood circle piece onto the felt, and trace around it with the marker. Use pinking shears to cut around the traced shape.

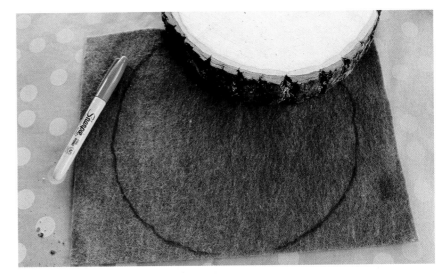

2. Center the felt piece onto the bottom side of the larger wood circle piece, and use heavy-duty adhesive to secure it in place. Set aside to dry for 30 minutes.

3 While the adhesive dries, use the paintbrush to apply two to three coats of the craft paint onto the wood candlestick, allowing the paint to dry for 15 minutes between coats. As you paint, leave the top and bottom of the candlestick unpainted, as these will not be visible in the finished project. Set the candlestick aside to dry completely, at least one hour.

4 Center the bottom of the candlestick onto the top of the larger wood circle piece, which will be the base of the finished pedestal. Affix the candlestick to the wood piece with heavy-duty adhesive, pressing firmly to secure.

5 Place the remaining wood piece so that it is centered on top of the candlestick, making sure the wood piece is precisely centered. Secure the wood piece to the candlestick with the heavy-duty adhesive. Set the completed pedestal aside until the adhesive is dry, approximately three hours.

6 When the adhesive is dry, cover the top and lower tiers of the pedestal with small sections of moss. Anchor the sections of moss to the piece with the heavy-duty adhesive to affix them permanently in place, or leave the sections of moss loose so they can be removed to create a new display with the pedestal later on.

7 Arrange various other natural elements over the layer of moss on the upper and lower tiers of the piece: stones, pinecones, sticks, etc. Finish by adding three flameless pillar candles to the arrangement. (NOTE: Due to the flammable nature of the elements in the centerpiece, do not use traditional wick candles, which pose a fire risk.)

Pompom Topiary Centerpiece

There is something so fun about pompoms, and I always find myself incorporating them into my designs. They are a way to add an instant pop of personality to just about every project—including centerpieces! This pompom topiary centerpiece is elegantly unique, and it is a great way to add decorative height to a display. This centerpiece would be a fantastic way to display table numbers at a dinner party, or a miniature version would be perfect to hold place cards. By using different color schemes, these topiaries can easily be adapted to suit any number of occasions or seasons!

To make this centerpiece, you will need:

* Wood candlestick
* Papier-mâché cone
* Wood finial
* Acrylic craft paint in coordinating colors
* Metallic acrylic craft paint

* Corrugated cardboard
* Scissors
* Paintbrushes
* Pompom trim
* Hot glue gun and glue sticks

1 Paint the wood candlestick with the craft paint using the paintbrush. Apply two or three coats for even coverage, allowing paint to dry 15 minutes between coats. Set the candlestick aside to dry completely.

2 Paint the papier-mâché cone with two or three coats of the coordinating craft paint color using the paintbrush, allowing to dry 15 minutes between coats. Set the cone aside to dry completely, about one hour.

3 Using a paintbrush, apply two or three coats of metallic paint to the finial, allowing the paint to dry 15 minutes between coats. Allow the paint to dry completely.

4 Trace around the bottom of the cone onto the cardboard, and use scissors to cut out the circle piece. Apply a generous amount of hot glue onto the top of the candlestick, and then affix the cardboard circle piece to the candlestick, positioning the circle so it is precisely centered on top of the candlestick. Press firmly to secure.

5 Apply a ring of hot glue around the outer perimeter of the cardboard circle. Affix the cone piece to the cardboard/candlestick base by positioning it over the glue, making sure it is precisely centered.

6 If necessary, trim away a bit of the tip of the cone so that the finial can fit properly. Apply a bit of hot glue inside the finial piece, and press it down over the top of the cone to secure.

7 Cut a piece of the pompom trim that is long enough to wrap around the base of the cone. Using hot glue, affix the pompom trim around the lower edge of the cone where it meets the candlestick base, concealing the cardboard layer as you go.

Mason Jar Luminary Centerpiece

When it comes to centerpieces, the gentle twinkle of a candle can instantly transform a display into something romantic and beautiful! Displayed individually or in a grouping, this mason jar luminary centerpiece exudes vintage charm, and it is one of my favorite affordable centerpiece options to produce lovely results on even the tightest budget.

To make this centerpiece, you will need:

* Mason jar

* Decoupage medium

* Liquid food coloring

* Wood dowel or craft stick

* Paper plate and paper towel

* Hot glue gun and glue sticks

* Jute cording

* Ribbon

* Rock salt

* Tea candle

1 Pour the decoupage medium into the bottom of the jar, filling the jar up about 1" with the medium. Add two or three drops of food coloring, and use a wood dowel or craft stick to stir the coloring into the decoupage medium until it is fully incorporated.

2 Swirl the jar around so that the decoupage medium coats the sides of the jar, turning the jar from side to side until the inside of the jar up to the rim is completely covered with the mixture.

3 Invert the jar onto a paper plate, and allow it to sit for one hour to drain the excess decoupage medium from the inside of the jar.

4 Discard the plate containing the excess decoupage medium that has drained, and wipe the top rim of the jar clean with a paper towel. Set the jar aside to allow the decoupage medium to harden completely.

5 Affix the jute cording to the mouth of the jar, wrapping the cording two or three times around, and securing with small dabs of hot glue as you wrap.

6 Tie a bow with the ribbon, and use hot glue to affix the bow to the center front of the jar, directly over the wrapped jute section.

7 Fill the bottom of the jar with 1" of rock salt, and place the tea candle inside. Although candles with a wick can be used in this centerpiece, electronic candles are by far the safest and easiest option.

Tiered Plate Photo Centerpiece

With four children, our family photos truly are some of my most prized possessions. This tiered plate photo centerpiece is the perfect way to turn those precious memories into an attractive display. I love the idea of making this centerpiece for a wedding or a graduation celebration to showcase favorite photos from across the years. The square shape of the wood plaques used here also makes this the perfect project for turning Instagram™ photos from your phone into a centerpiece to enjoy in your home!

To make this centerpiece, you will need:

* Large plate for bottom tier
* Small plate for top tier
* Candlestick
* Heavy-duty adhesive
* Small square wood plaques
* Acrylic craft paint
* Paintbrushes

* Stencils
* Photos
* Paper trimmer or ruler and scissors
* Decoupage medium
* Rock salt
* Miscellaneous embellishments

1 Using the heavy-duty adhesive, affix the candlestick to the top center of the large plate, pressing firmly to secure. Set aside until the adhesive dries slightly, about 30 minutes.

2 Apply heavy-duty adhesive around the top rim of the candlestick, and then affix the small plate on top of the candlestick, making sure the top plate is precisely centered over the bottom plate. Set the piece aside to allow the adhesive to dry completely.

3 Use a paintbrush to apply the acrylic paint to all sides of the wood plaque pieces. To avoid waste, it is necessary only to paint the outer border of the front side of each plaque, as the center will be covered with a photo later on. Allow the paint to dry for 30 minutes, or until dry to the touch.

4 Stencil designs onto the back side of the wood plaques using a paintbrush and a contrasting color of acrylic paint. Allow the design to dry completely, about one hour.

5 Using a paper trimmer or a ruler and scissors, trim the photos so they are about ¼" smaller on all sides than the wood plaque pieces.

6 Working with one plaque at a time, use a paintbrush to apply decoupage medium to the front side of the plaque. Apply a thin layer of the decoupage medium to the back side of one of the photos.

7 Working quickly, center the photo over the plaque piece, and press down to secure, using your fingers to smooth out any bubbles underneath. Use the brush to apply a thin layer of the decoupage medium over the photo, focusing especially on the outer edges of the photo. Set the piece aside to dry completely. Repeat Steps 6–7 with the remaining photos and wood plaques.

8 Pour a thin layer of rock salt into the top and bottom tiers of the plate stand, and then nestle the completed photo plaques into the salt on both tiers of the stand so they stand upright. If desired, embellish further with a decorative wood word accent or other small ornament.

Hot Air Balloon Centerpiece

Paper lanterns are such a fun item to work with, and they can give any project a playful, happy vibe. This hot air balloon centerpiece is truly one of my favorites, since it has plenty of whimsical impact but is so surprisingly easy to make. A rainbow of these would be perfect for a child's birthday party or for a baby shower, or even as a clever addition to the decor for a going-away party.

To make this centerpiece, you will need:

* 10" paper lantern
* 4" round papier-mâché box
* ¼" x 12" wood dowels (4)
* Acrylic craft paint
* Paintbrushes
* Floral foam

* Scissors
* Pompom trim
* Rickrack trim
* Jute cording
* Hot glue
* Shredded paper filler

1. Using a paintbrush, paint the outside of the papier-mâché box with the craft paint, applying two or three coats for even coverage, allowing the paint to dry for 15 minutes between coats. Set aside to dry completely.

2. Insert the wood dowels down into a square piece of floral foam, and apply two to three coats of paint to each one. Allow to dry completely.

3 Cut a piece of the pompom trim that is long enough to wrap around the papier-mâché box. Affix the trim to the box with hot glue so the top edge of the trim piece is aligned with the top rim of the box.

4 Trim one or two pieces of the rickrack trim long enough to wrap around the circumference of the paper lantern. Affix the trim piece(s) to the lantern with hot glue.

5 Cut a piece of foam that fits snugly into the bottom of the papier-mâché box. The top of the foam piece should be about 1" lower than the top rim of the box. Insert the wood dowels into the foam inside the box so they are evenly spaced around the outer perimeter of the box.

6 Using sharp scissors, poke four small, evenly spaced holes along the lower edge of the lantern. Insert one of the wood dowels up and through each hole, and secure with a small dab of hot glue.

7 Make four small bows from the jute cording, and affix them over the four points where the lantern and wood dowels meet.

8 Fill the empty space above the foam piece in the papier-mâché box with the shredded paper filler to conceal the foam and dowel ends.

Dipped Bottle Centerpiece

Empty bottles are such a fantastic idea for centerpiece projects. They can so quickly and easily be dressed up into a pretty vase, as is the case here with this lovely dipped bottle centerpiece. With just a bit of spray paint and some other basic supplies, a simple glass bottle is transformed into a display that is elegant enough for a formal event—but without having to make a huge investment of time or money!

To make this centerpiece, you will need:

* Empty glass bottle
* White spray paint
* Liquid gilding
* Paintbrush
* Decorative metal trim
* Scissors

* Heavy-duty adhesive
* Feather pick
* Two-sided paper
* Paper trimmer
* Hot glue gun and glue sticks
* ½" circle paper punch

1 Spray two or three coats of the spray paint onto the outside surface of the glass bottle, allowing the paint to dry for 15 minutes between coats. To prevent dripping, apply the paint in very light coats, keeping the nozzle of the paint can at least eight inches from the bottle as you spray. Set the bottle aside to dry completely.

2 Use the paintbrush to apply a rim of the liquid gilding around the lower edge of the bottle to give the project a metallic-dipped effect. Set the bottle aside to allow the gilding to dry completely.

3 Use scissors to cut a piece of the metal trim that is long enough to wrap around the mouth of the bottle. Affix the trim to the bottle with the heavy-duty adhesive.

4 Insert the feather pick stem-side down into the bottle.

5 Use the paper trimmer to cut a strip of paper that is 1" wide and 12" long. Starting at one of the narrow ends, fold the piece accordion style until you reach the opposite narrow end of the piece.

6 Overlap the ends of the strip to form a loop and secure with hot glue at the point where the ends overlap.

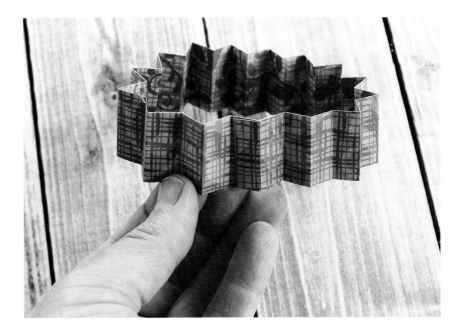

7 Use the paper punch to create two ½" circle pieces. Press the accordion paper loop piece flat on a work surface to form a circular medallion shape, and then affix a punched circle piece to the front and back center of the medallion to hold it in shape.

8 Position the medallion piece as desired on the front of the bottle just beneath the metal trim, and secure it with hot glue.

Tasseled Tree Branch Centerpiece

Nature is full of things that can serve as the foundation for a terrific centerpiece! In this tasseled tree branch centerpiece, a bit of paint and some handmade tassels transform a humble tree branch into a display brimming with color and texture. This particular centerpiece can be made as large or as small as you need, making it perfect for a wide variety of occasions. And as an added bonus, the tassels here are so quick and fun to make, they are perfect for stringing onto a garland or even tying onto a wrapped gift.

To make this centerpiece, you will need:

* Tree branch
* Mason jar
* Spray paint
* Sandpaper
* Floral foam
* Rock salt

* Paper flowers
* Hot glue gun and glue sticks
* Tissue paper
* Scissors
* Washi tape

1 Apply two or three coats of spray paint to the tree branch, and set it aside to dry completely. Spray paint the outside of the mason jar, applying the paint in light, even coats to prevent the paint from dripping. Allow the jar to dry completely before using sandpaper to sand off some of the paint for a distressed look.

2 Cut a piece of floral foam to fit down inside the jar while leaving about 3" of space between the top of the foam and the top rim of the jar. Tuck the branch down into the foam, and fill the space above the foam with rock salt to conceal the base of the branch.

3 For each tassel, cut a 10" square piece of tissue paper. Lay the piece flat on a work surface, and fold the bottom edge up to meet the top edge, so the piece is folded in half.

4 Fold the left edge over to meet the right edge, making sure all raw edges and corners are aligned and the piece is shaped like a square. Fold the left edge over once again to meet the right edge and press firmly to crease the fold, so the piece is now shaped like a rectangle.

5 Use scissors to make vertical cuts about ¼" apart, starting at the unfolded short edge of the rectangle and ending about 1" from the short folded edge. Unfold the entire piece and cut it into four equal sections, cutting from one fringed edge up to the other fringed edge.

6 Working with one section at a time, lay the piece flat down on a work surface and, starting along one of the long edges, roll it up tightly to form a tube.

7 Twist the uncut center section of the rolled piece tightly, and then fold the piece in half so that the fringed ends are aligned at the bottom and there is a twisted loop at the top.

8 Wrap a piece of washi tape just under the loop to secure the tassel. Repeat Steps 4–8 to make tassels from the remaining sections before hanging them throughout the tree branch. Use hot glue to affix the paper flowers to the tips of the tree branch, scattering the flowers evenly throughout.

Felt Flower Centerpiece

I love to bring bright, bold color into my craft projects! This felt flower centerpiece is brimming with vibrant hues and great texture, and it is a wonderful way to have a floral element in a display without having to worry about live plants. These felt flowers are so simply made, and they can be done in any color you choose in order to fit the mood you want to create: bold and bright for a birthday or anniversary celebration, or perhaps soft and romantic for a wedding or baby shower. The choice is completely up to you!

To make this centerpiece, you will need:

- Terracotta pot and saucer
- White and black acrylic craft paint
- Paintbrushes
- Foam brush
- Painter's tape
- Chalkboard medium

- Chalk
- Styrofoam™ ball that fits snugly inside the pot
- Serrated knife
- Wool felt in assorted colors
- Scissors
- Hot glue gun and glue sticks

1 Paint the entire outer surface of the terracotta pot and saucer with the white craft paint using the paintbrush, applying two or three coats as needed for even coverage. Set the pot and saucer aside to dry completely, about one hour.

2 Affix the painter's tape around the pot to form a ring around the middle. Use the paintbrush to apply the black paint inside the taped-off section, applying two or three coats for even coverage. Allow the paint to dry completely, about one hour. Do not remove the painter's tape.

3 Use the foam brush to apply two coats of the chalkboard medium over the black paint layer, allowing the chalkboard medium to dry for one hour between coats. Set aside to dry completely. Once dry, remove the painter's tape, and write a desired message within the border with a piece of chalk.

4 Use the serrated knife to cut the Styrofoam ball in half. Place one of the halves, cut side down, inside the pot. Press firmly to secure in place.

5 Use the scissors to cut a 3" and a 1½" circle from the wool felt. Set the smaller piece aside. Starting along one of the outer edges, cut the 3" piece in a spiral until you reach the center of the piece.

6 Starting at the center of the spiral and working toward the outside, roll the felt piece to create a rosette shape.

7 Working carefully to avoid burns, secure the outer tip of the spiral to the body of the flower with a dab of hot glue.

8 Apply a generous amount of hot glue to the back side of the flower, making sure all of the sections of the spiral are covered with the glue.

9 Working quickly, affix the 1½" felt circle to the back of the flower, pressing firmly to secure. This will hold all of the layers of the flower in place. Repeat Steps 5–9 to create as many flowers as needed to cover the entire surface of the Styrofoam ball.

10 Use hot glue to affix the flowers to the Styrofoam ball, placing the flowers close together so the foam is not visible between the flowers. Continue until the entire surface of the ball is covered.

11 Use the scissors to cut five or six green leaf shapes. Affix the leaves between some of the flower pieces using hot glue.